SH-BOOM!

The Power of Positive Aging

by

Douglas A. Cox

SH-BOOM! The Power of Postive Aging

Douglas A. Cox
1000 N. Green Valley Parkway
Suite 440-392
Henderson, NV 89074
United States of America
Website: DougCoxOnline.com
Email: Doug@DougCoxOnline.com

Illustrations by Christopher Cox
Photography by Denis Bancroft
Editing by Sharon Norman
Book Layout & Design by Linda A. Bell, BellCreativeStudio.com

SELF-HELP / Personal Growth / Happiness: sh-boom, the power of positive aging / Douglas A. Cox -1st. ed.

ISBN-13: 978-1536983838
ISBN-10: 1536983837

Printed in the United States of America

CONTENTS

INTRODUCTION
To The Adventure

If you are between the ages of 50-100, this is your time and this is your book!

This book is for and about Sh-Boomers! Who? A Sh-Boomer is anyone between the ages of 50-100! We are the largest and most powerful group of humanity who ever lived. We may be young or old, depending on how we are handling this adventure called aging. Sh-Boomers are explorers, making our way courageously into a world where we have never gone before. We are feeling pain where none existed; we find diminishing hearing, eyesight, and memory where sound, vision, and recall were once crystal clear. Our bodies make noises when we stand up and our movements are a bit slower than they once were. At the same time, we have the opportunity to be discovering an abundance of joy and pleasure that the young are still "experiencing" but have no way of processing.

The fireworks on the cover of this book are a reminder that a new idea, a new experience, or a treasured memory is the explosion of joy within the fireworks of our infinite minds. Sh-Boom!

Come with me... eyes open, mind open... wide open!

Whether we are empowered by age or enfeebled by it is in great measure up to us!

By reading about one of my fellow travelers perhaps you will come to know your author in the process. What I learned from this, one of my many colleagues and mentors, explains a great deal about this book. Enjoy...

Preparing to present an inspirational seminar for a group of 300 professionals, I found myself in a hotel above the hot springs in Arkansas, meditating on the message for the day. As I often do, I turned on the news, making a final check, to be sure I hadn't missed some event that would cause me embarrassment in front of the audience. I immediately realized it was Sunday.

Sunday in the South... meant that every channel would have a preacher of some stripe, pouring forth his or her message. The first of the three channels I found was commanded by a screamer, which has never been my cup of good book, so I switched to the next, only to find a dreary pastor who nearly put me to sleep during the first sentence. I moved onto my third and final choice... and my patience was rewarded! Out onto the small screen walked a man of modest stature but obvious self-assurance. His short white hair stood out against his dark turtleneck, and as he turned to face me and his huge congregation, he spoke in a most unassuming and respectful voice.

"Today," he said modestly, "I am going to preach a sermon that's only going to take fifteen minutes." He paused while a smattering of laughter went throughout the unseen congregation and then he went on. "Now I had some friends ask me how I could possibly deliver a sermon in fifteen minutes and I answered... because I'm only going to tell you what I know..." The laughter began in earnest! "I'm not going to tell you what I think..." and then softly he added, "just what I know."

In the next fifteen minutes I laughed until I cried and cried until I laughed and I realized that I had heard one of the great human beings and messengers of our time. He was so real, so modest, and so respectful of his faith and his position on that stage in front of the world that he drew us to him and made us a part of his message. I have never been a joiner but that day I decided to send a little money each month to support his ministry, and, of course, I ordered a dozen copies of his sermon on CD. It was titled, "What everyone gives that nobody wants!"

In that hotel room, on that Sunday morning, I made the decision to figure out how to meet this wonderful man and share a friendship with him. It wasn't easy making a connection with one of the world's truly great ministers. I was only one of millions who hoped for that audience, but it was worth the time and effort to make it happen.

One of my original Ten Challenges says, "Educate yourself by communicating with those who can teach you the most!" It took years to accomplish this meeting, but recently I stood shoulder to shoulder with this great man, in the same huge chapel where he had delivered his fifteen-minute sermon on the day that I first experienced the joy of hearing Dr. Gerald Mann speak. Our time together, riding on a golf cart around the beautiful grounds of the Riverbend Church in Austin, Texas, was pure enjoyment and our lunch together at Chili's Restaurant, along with the hug that concluded our precious visit, was an answer to my prayers and a blessed opportunity to visit with my hero, my mentor, and now my friend.

Dr. Gerald Mann left this earthly life in 2015.

Please enjoy my book. It is an easy read, because I'm only going to tell you what I know... not what I think!

CHAPTER ONE
About Us

For all of the nearly eight decades of my life, I have tried hard to live in the Now. Not wishing to be younger or hankering to get older, but fully alive right here, right now. I not only wanted to live in the moment but I wanted to find greater and greater joy in the time of life in which I found myself. Here on my journey, I am continuing to discover the secrets of a peaceful, healthy, strong and wealthy, Sh-boomer life. Lest you may be laboring under a misconception, I was not born healthy, wealthy, or wise. I have shared nearly every tragedy that one can endure and it is exactly these challenges in life that have awakened my spirit, filled me with courage, and helped to strengthen my resolve to enjoy this journey called life.

Now it is your turn to begin to spend that joy you have stashed away for just this occasion. Here are the secrets of cashing in your "401-A-OK" plan for celebrating the moment and leading the world that follows you. If you have ever reached out to find and recapture the joy of life that seems to have slipped away, perhaps the gateway to that path is here before you. Here you may read, digest, absorb, keep, or discard the ideas contained in this little book. Every word has been lived, tested, and shaped in life's crucible. Following these simple steps, you may become part of the never-ending Sh-Boomer story!

Can you come out to play? An Explosion of Joy awaits you!

Hey, hey we're Sh-Boomers... 50-55-60-65-70-75-80-85-90-95-100

Here we come, ready or not!

CHAPTER TWO
The Power Of My Dream

The opening line of the song, "Sh-Boom," reads: "Life could be a dream..." Whether you heard it as I did by the original group, The Chords, or later on by the Crew Cuts, or more recently in the fantastic computer animated film Cars, the song is a musical memory that never quite fades away. At a recent dinner with beloved friends and family, I sent up a test balloon for my book title. When the song "Sh-Boom" was mentioned, all ages and personalities around the table began to sing the song. The Sh-Boomers, Boomers, Millennials, Xers, and Yers confirmed that I had chosen the perfect title, "Sh-Boom!" It calls to mind the power of dreams, the joy of love, and the rhythm and music of days gone by. Perhaps, more importantly, it sings out to the hopes of days yet to come.

Today I will renew my mind by practicing the art of "dreaming." Dreams are ageless and timeless. I will begin by calling to mind the names of men and women who came before me, who had the courage to dream, regardless of their ages, situations, and conditions. I am not finished, but just beginning. Greatness has no age limitation. That which I can dream, I can accomplish. As a cartographer prepares a map for the journey of a lifetime, I will write my thoughts, dreams, and wishes on a blank piece of paper. I will fold my "Dreamsheet" and keep it with me as a focus point for my Dreams when I become distracted by life's challenges. Most importantly, my Dreamsheet will become a reminder of my increasing worth to myself, family, and to society.

I have a Dream!

My Two Cents...

Ever since I read the story of King Arthur and saw the play Camelot, I have been fascinated by the romance and magic of the tale. I was intrigued by the counsel given to the king by his friend and teacher, Merlin. Until then, I didn't know that wizards remember forward and that is how they can see and so, predict the future. Not knowing any better, I immediately began to emulate the teaching of the wise old man.

Want to give it a try? Take a few quiet moments for yourself and find a place to sit, undisturbed. Bring along a plain, blank piece of paper and a pen and then think ahead...

What is it you want, Arthur? What are the things that you most wish to accomplish? How do you see yourself, your kingdom, and your people in the days to come? In simple terms and brief sentences, inscribe your hopes and dreams on the document before you. Don't concern yourself now with the size of the round table or the names of the knights who will come to join you on your quest; just begin the process.

Does it work? For the last fifty years I have been imagining my future and then doing whatever it takes to turn those dreams into realities. Although you will not be writing in quill pen and ink on pure parchment, the inspiration and the timeless laws of success await your command. By the sword, Excalibur, I will do this!

Wherever you are in life, someone is going to determine your future. Why shouldn't that someone be you?

PERSONAL JOURNAL

On this page you may make notes about the things you would like most to accomplish in your life. Keep it simple here. Once you have experienced the book at least once, at the end you will find a complete guideline for creating a thorough, powerful, personal Dreamsheet!

CHAPTER THREE
The Magic Of Believing

Today I will begin to restore my energy and power by reawakening my willingness and ability to believe. I realize that to believe in others and then in life, I must first rekindle my belief in myself and my dreams at a higher level. I need to work on dispelling the reasons that things can't happen; remove that "t," go for the "can," and hold on to the magic that is mine to command. Although sometimes I may see signs that civilization is not as civil as it once was back in the day, I will search faithfully and tirelessly for positive and worthwhile things in others and in life. I will remember that somewhere, within a mile of my home, a boy scout is accepting his eagle award, a ninety-five-year-old woman is onstage receiving her college diploma, and an impoverished child is in the front row of a classroom, struggling through an exam that will open up the possibilities that only education can provide.

I will not allow the evening news to become my birdcage. I will know and remember that for every shocking report of crime and violence I see or read about, there are also many wonderful things being accomplished all around me. "Breaking News" is not designed to promote your well being! It is designed to benefit the broadcasters and the advertisers. I will hold on to not only the "better angels of my nature," but the higher nature in others as well. I will choose to believe in myself, my nation, and what is still so good and right with the world. "Ain't no mountain high enough!"

Fear and trepidation do not simply disappear; they are replaced with true and valuable information.

My Two Cents...

In the Southwest Airlines boarding terminal—gate 3—I sat, awaiting my turn to board flight 266 from FLL to LAS. From my seat, I had a clear view of the concourse and passengers scurrying from one place to another. I saw a tiny bird, a house finch I believe, flying down from the support beams fifty feet in the air and landing on the worn carpet, searching for scraps from the diners. It seemed that she had found a perfect home in the world of humans. She had food, shelter, and some safety from predators. Sounds like an easy life, right?

As she flew back and forth, past the windows that looked out onto the world, I wondered if she ever looked out and saw the incredible possibilities just outside of her self-imposed cage. Perhaps she just didn't "believe" what she was seeing out there.

No matter how large, whether real or imagined, a cage is still a cage. Never allow yourself to be any less than all you can be. Instead of looking for reasons to complain, look for reasons to celebrate. Don't give up, keep looking and keep exploring, wondering and practicing the magic of believing!

As we begin to see more in ourselves, we will surely see more in others. What a gift!

As far as you can see, as much as you can imagine, as great as you can dream, so must you also believe!

PERSONAL JOURNAL

Give yourself a terrific and precious gift! Make a list here of those things in which you truly believe. You may wish to start with your faith, but then you must continue on to add those things that bring comfort, courage, and sustenance to your life. I always try to begin with the words "I Believe" and then let the responses flow.

CHAPTER FOUR
The Sense Of Honor

Today I will reawaken the sense of honor that I have hidden away in the darkened closet of my mind. I will recall not just the honor for God and country and family with which I was raised, but the honor of word and deed. However alone I seem at times, someone is always watching, always aware of my communications and actions. I will stand or sit as straight as my body will allow and speak with confidence about the many positive things that I have learned during my lifetime. I will salute the glories of my generation, laugh at the follies and foolishness of my time, and be a positive example. Whether at the ball field, rodeo arena, or in my own living room, I will remove my hat and place my hand over my heart at the playing of our national anthem. I will remember the words and sing along, even if I sing alone. Though each generation has its own ways, I will, in my way, set an example of long held, timeless traditions that give others reason to welcome and look forward to the passage of time.

Yes! Those are tears of respect!

My Two Cents...

When I was twelve-years-old I was given the opportunity to audition for the Pasadena Boy Choir. It was a very important moment for me, because my older brother (and hero) had been the lead soprano soloist in the choir for some years. I was accepted and as the months and years passed by, we rehearsed, improved, and performed throughout Southern California. At Christmastime we sang in nearly every large department store. It was quite a sight to see seventy-five cherubic-appearing choir boys descending Macy's escalator, all in our freshly pressed choir robes, holding our hymn books before us and singing like angels. It was a major commitment in time and energy to learn the songs, practice the harmony, and perform on the weekends when our friends were playing football. I loved every minute of it!

One Easter we were invited to perform in the beautiful chapel at Forest Lawn in Glendale, California. We filed onto our risers and into our rows, awaiting the arrival of our choir master and director, John Henry Lyons. He appeared before us, looked over his glasses at us, and raised his baton. There is a magic to the purity of boys' voices in the days just before they begin to change. It is a sweet, spiritual sound and our performance that day was as perfect as could be. Our closing was a very simple, rich version of "Now the Day Is Over" and when we came to the end, Dr. Lyons led us in a Dresden Amen. It is a beautiful repeating of the word amen, in which our voices built to a crescendo, filling the chapel with the sound of our devotion. For a moment I thought about all of our voices and realized that it wouldn't matter if I stopped singing. After all, mine was just one voice. And then, in that holy place, it became clear to me that without my voice, the sound, the resonance in that cathedral, would never have been quite the same.

You must think, listen, and speak. You must practice and sing. You must add your voice to the chorus of human kind. Without your one voice, the richness of the composition of life can never be complete.

Always remember: whether it is a vocal or a vote, your one voice truly matters!

PERSONAL JOURNAL

On this Personal Journal page, I suggest that you write as a historian of your life and times, about those things that filled you with a sense of honor. Do not limit your thinking and writing to big things alone. We are best remembered not for the big things done occasionally, but the little things done consistently.

CHAPTER FIVE
I Will Celebrate

Today I will celebrate! I will list those simple or wonderful accomplishments of my life and the many little things that I have done for others. I will not wait for birthdays, parties, events, or others to join me. I will, within myself, simply celebrate. Though some of my friends have fallen in the course of health and time and tragedy, I will remember their spoken and written words and kindness shared as if they were still here. For me they will never be gone.

Though their passing touches me, I will remember how Dudley Moore's Arthur Bach exclaimed, "I was lucky to have known him at all." Although the style and art of personal communication may have changed around us,

I will, with perhaps shaky penmanship, write and send greeting cards to those I care about, especially those who may receive none. I will faithfully sign and send thank-you notes to those who have shown the simplest kindness for me and for others. What an easy and wonderful way to acknowledge another's caring and show appreciation. I will not try to be the life of the party, but instead celebrate the party of life.

In the southwestern part of America, there is a beautiful tradition, Noches de las Luminarias (pronounced No-chase day las Loomin-ah- re-ahs); in Spanish it means, "The nights of the festival lights." It is a custom during the holidays in which pathways and entryways to churches, gardens, and homes, such as ours, are lighted to *celebrate* the arrival of guests. The lanterns, luminarias or farolitos, as they are called, are created by placing candles on sand in paper bags and placing them as guideposts along the walkways. Once you have seen these wonderful dancing lights, you will not forget their glow.

There are many holiday traditions that I wish would be kept throughout the year; kindness, respect, honor, and love among others. Is it not possible that we might let our light shine in such a way that we could become a guide for the lost, a rest for the weary, support for the ailing, and perhaps a candle in the wind for strangers who pass our way? Of course it's possible. I know, because I have friends and family who cast just such a glow every day of the year. I want to be more like them.

My Two Cents...

Celebration... it's a feeling, it's a song, it's an expression, and it's a way of life; it may also be a measure of our health and longevity. I have lived so much of my life "happy" that it has taken me a while to convince my kids that I have been touched by sadness, too.

I once did a sales/inspiration training for a large group of people in the corporate world. During the class we laughed and cheered, learned and practiced, ran around and shared a day-long energetic experience. The event went so well that the sales took a tremendous leap and I was invited to become an ongoing part of that company's programs.

About a year later at another gathering of that same group, one of the original students came up to me and asked to share what she thought might be an embarrassing confidence. I love feedback and so I said absolutely! She revealed that during my original presentation, the group had gotten together to try to figure out where my energy came from and just why I was so happy all the time. She said that they hatched a plan to keep me occupied with questions, while one of them went to the back of the room and went through my jacket... looking for drugs! (They didn't find any.) It is sad to think that happiness, even amidst the challenges of life, needs to be drug induced. We have all been touched by illness, tragedy, and loss. I am convinced that it is how we come through these storms that marks us for success and well being. Happiness may be one of the greatest forms of worship.

PERSONAL JOURNAL

On this page begin the process of listing family members, friends, and acquaintances with whom you wish to connect or re-connect. Remember to include births, birthdays, anniversaries, graduations, meetings, accomplishments, and passings. Though you may be quite computer savvy, for the purpose of this process, use longhand to collect these precious memories. Writing is becoming a lost art. Picasso and Rembrandt would not have been masters without putting brush to canvas. The art of writing, in longhand, is a way of seeing the collaboration of your head and heart, which creates a permanent memory of these things.

Remember... we Sh-Boomers have our own secret code... it's called cursive!

CHAPTER SIX
Today I Will Be Thankful

Our bodies change and are shaped by time, but no matter how my outside changes, it is still me in here! Just because I do not look and feel like I did when I was nineteen is no reason to let the world keep me back or hold me down. I may give out, but I will never give up! There was a time when I was proud of my pain from a workout or a marathon or a game. Today I will look upon my life as a great game or adventure in which I have played the starring role, run the race, lifted the burdens, and helped my team to victory. I will think of my aches and pains as a badge of courage for a game well played. I will dine for both fuel and fun. I will eat wisely, breathe deeply, and relax. In my stillness, I will meditate, learn, and practice the art of blocking the aches and pains that may come. I am enough just as I am. Every day is a new beginning, a fresh adventure, an opportunity to believe in myself, my dreams, and all of the possibilities life has to offer.

My Two Cents...

Valentine's Day morning was a wonder here in Las Vegas. When I began my daily walk up the mountain, it was seventy-four degrees under a cloudless, turquoise sky.

As I neared the crest of the trail, I saw two hikers coming down. When we came within ten feet of each other, I said "Howdy..." No response. Nearly everyone shares greetings on Doug's Mountain, so this seemed strange. Then the answer became clear.

Face-to-face, the man reached out and touched my shoulder. Without a word he began to mime a warning of the treacherous trail up ahead. He pretended to use a walking stick and then acted like he was about to lose his balance and fall. Not knowing my familiarity of the climb, he was sharing with me the dangers of the last part of the trail. He and his companion were deaf and mute. They were certainly great communicators.

I wanted to tell him thanks, but for the life of me I couldn't remember the sign for thank you. We shared a smile and I passed them by on the trail. At twenty feet distance I turned up-trail to face them once again. I waited until they were looking my way and I drew an imaginary big heart on my red lifeguard sweatshirt. Then I made the sign for "I love you" and held my hand in the middle of my chest.

They smiled until I thought that their faces would crack.

It is truly hard to be grumpy with a mouthful of thank you!

PERSONAL JOURNAL

Jack was in the automobile business. There wasn't anything about cars that he did not know. We never bought or leased a vehicle without seeking his counsel. During a hospital visit for a procedure that seemed trivial, something went very wrong and our friend Jack became paralyzed from the waist down. He never let the challenge dissuade him from the wonderful life he had been living. As Jack always exclaimed, arriving cheerfully in his hot-rod wheelchair, "As long as it's my butt and not my brain that is in this chair, I am doing alright!" On this very special Personal Journal page, begin to list the many things for which you can be thankful. I call them blessings. During health issue days, this will not be the easiest of tasks and yet with attitude on high and mind open, you can find a sense of growing joy in your gratefulness.

Although you may do so as often as you wish, make it your commitment to add to this list on a weekly basis.

CHAPTER SEVEN
Today I Will Accept The Compliment

Today I will look at the nation around me, the buildings, the bridges, the highways, and all of the many accomplishments of my time and be proud that I was a part of all of this. It matters not if I held a hammer, lifted a shovel, or carried a rifle; I am one who, through my labors and faithful service, supported all of these amazing gifts of our centuries. Many of us grew up in a family or a time when celebrating our accomplishments was looked upon as arrogance or conceit. But it does not become us to discount the person giving us the compliment. It doesn't take long to alter the behavior and genuine kindness offered by others when we regularly dismiss or disregard their compliments.

When offered a compliment or a thank you, too many of us go into our "Aw Shucks" routine and begin to kick rocks or shuffle our feet. It is time for us Sh-Boomers to learn and practice using the marvelous words, "You're Welcome!" Please notice that I did not use the popular term, "No Problem..." It is not a substitute for You're Welcome. It is my fondest wish that I was not a problem for you! Men, women and children; when that hand comes out to thank you, grab on with enthusiasm and respond, "You're Welcome!"

My Two Cents...

"Heroes and Friends"; that's the title of a song written by Randy Travis and Don Schlitz.

When I first saw the YouTube video of Randy in this recording session, I was reminded of how many folks have contributed to my life in so many ways. During the video, the image of Roy Rogers appeared in the window of the recording studio and I understood exactly what Randy was singing about: "Your heroes will help you find good in yourself..."

How often the compliments and constructive criticisms of both new and old friends have helped to put me back in the saddle, a better man. "Your friends won't forsake you for somebody else..." How faithfully both family and friends have stuck with me on the bumpy trail up this mountain we call life.

Okay, Sh-Boomers, wherever you find yourself on the trail these days, google "Heroes and Friends," by Randy Travis and share the experience. Take a few moments and let yourself out of the corral. For each of us, there is a face in the window of the recording studio who you know has ridden or would ride to the ends of the earth with you.

To my friends, I'm reaching out to tell you that you are my heroes and sheroes and I truly appreciate your friendship! For my readers, I am honored to say that We Ride Together.

The years have gone by, but now and again my heart rides the range with my heroes and friends...

PERSONAL JOURNAL

"Through the years," as Kenny Rogers sings; from time to time, we have been given sincere compliments by those we know. Often, without realizing it, we have diminished the importance of our discourse with those who care for us and wish to honor our contribution. When we fail to graciously acknowledge a genuine compliment, we are saying "your words, your thoughts don't matter."

Make a "thank you" list here.

CHAPTER EIGHT
I Will Remember

Today I will remember on a whole new level. I will reminisce about the music and songs that have made my life what it is today. I will begin by making a list of my favorite songs. I will include the songs to which I fell in love, songs that made me get up and dance, songs that awakened my laughter and songs that brought me to tears, but most of all, I will list the music that has inspired me to think and feel. From Handel to Hendrix, Mozart to Miller, Beethoven to The Beatles and Sidney Bechet to The Beach Boys, I will find this music among my records or CDs or I will have a friend help me find these treasures and save them as an audio file. I will keep them and play them often.

I will begin, starting with my favorite lines, to memorize every word in every song. On going to my rest each night, I will say my prayers and then fall asleep repeating my chosen line for the day, until new grooves are carved into my seasoned gray matter and new cells are generated in my infinite mind. I will remember these songs, because this is the soundtrack of my life. I will allow myself the great "Goose Pimple Quotient"! As the hair on my arms rise with the ebb and flow of the music, I will realize that "G.P.Q." is the measurement of how alive I am and always will be, in the music and memories of my life.

I remember: the smell of freshly washed linen hanging on the clothesline; teaberry, licorice, and clove chewing gum; the sound of a squeaky screen door opening; or a friend riding over on a bicycle with playing cards in the spokes. I remember the five-and-dime store, service stations where the attendant checked my oil, filled my gas tank, and washed my windows. I still love BB guns and I recall clearly the sounds at a soda fountain and the ice cold silver milkshake container, with always just a little extra in the bottom. I remember the Ed Sullivan Show and the many stars he brought into our homes. I remember the cathedral radio that sat in our living room and introduced us to Sargent Preston, The Green Hornet, The Shadow, Fibber McGee and Molly, and my favorite, The Lone Ranger. I treasure these fond memories, but as the "daring and resourceful masked rider of the plains" taught us, we do not need these things for our lives to go Sh-Boom. At whatever age... we can still be daring and resourceful!

"I remember America," as my friend John Stewart sings.

My Two Cents...

Do you own some old 45 or 78 RPM records? If so, why? Why do they matter to you? Why do you keep records that you can no longer play?

My friend, Ian Gavet, posted something on Facebook that got me thinking... why do we keep these relics and why do we remember these songs and lyrics? The answer is, because they are a very real part of our hearts and history. When I was in the radio and recording business, I met some famous folks and it was a pleasure. Today, I remember the artists and writers whose voices, music, and recordings were never given a chance; the artists who put their lives and souls into songs that they believed would be the next big hit. I would like to share one such story.

"Falling in Love Again," by Ted Mulry, was a song sent to me by a friend from RCA records in Australia. I liked the 70s song and agreed to try to get it played on the radio. We got it started in Southern California and audiences seemed to love the song. Imagine my surprise when I was told by the record company to stop promoting it. All I could think about was the disappointment in the heart of my new friend Ted Mulry, who had his hopes and dreams spinning around at 45 RPM on that little piece of vinyl. You can Google "Falling in Love Again" by Ted Mulry. We lost Ted in 2001, but like so many of the priceless treasures of our times, his music lives on. Perhaps we are all a bit Ted Mulry, believing that our hit is just around the corner.

Meet me in the gym... kick off your shoes and save me a dance...

PERSONAL JOURNAL

On this page put down some recollections of your favorite recordings. What was your favorite radio station? Who was your favorite deejay? What was your favorite kind of music and why? In the rhythm, lyrics, and music of these oldies we may well find not only the memories of our days gone by, but the possibilities of our future mental health as well.

CHAPTER NINE
I Will Develop My Sense of Humor

Today I will laugh all over again. Humor may be more than just the best medicine; it may also be the best IQ test ever. It's amazing but true that tragedy and humor have about the same shelf life in our memories. Once again I will prove how bright I am by thinking of playground jokes, funny moments, and foolish things that I have done. I will laugh out loud, no matter what the others think. I will listen to Bob Newhart, Flip Wilson, Jeff Foxworthy, Jonathon Winters, Ellen DeGeneres, and John Pinette and realize how funny they are and still can be without four-letter words. I will Google routines by Carol Burnett, Tim Conway, and Harvey Korman and watch and laugh until the tears run down my leg. I will listen to and practice the

39

comedy routine, "Who's on first," until I can recite it from memory. I will keep alive the wonderful, funny things that I have heard and repeat them, if only to myself. My friend Mason Williams wrote some poetry that I still remember, word for word: "Lunch Toters," "Moose Goosers," "Tummy Gummers," and "Toad Suckers," to name just a few. These rhymes will send you running for the bathroom with laughter.

Whatever my taste in music, once in a while I will tune in to a country station and listen to some great country songs that have a fine way of looking and laughing at life. For example, the recent "Red Neck Yacht Club"! By Craig Morgan or "Ocean Front Property," by George Strait and "Rye Whiskey," recorded in 1936 by Tex Ritter, the father of John Ritter. I will watch the goings-on around me and observe the funny things that people do and call it life.

There is no medicine for pain, like real, deep laughter. The more it hurts, the more I will laugh. Those of you who have attended my presentations know that on stage, my humor is always on me. As Red Skelton taught, I do not make jokes at the expense of others. Laughter is an incredible doorway between us...

My Two Cents...

I love to speak at high schools. Although it's not the easiest task that I have chosen, it is one of the most rewarding. I have spoken to thousands of teenagers all across the country. I believe that my success at these events is based on two postulates. First, I don't go out to teach these young wizards, I go onstage to learn from them. And second, I am aware of how humans, of any age, want so desperately to find a common place in which to connect.

For a moment, imagine yourself to be a thirteen- to seventeen-year-old young adult, sitting in an auditorium or multipurpose room, shoulder-to-shoulder with others who feel just like you. You act aggressively to hide your shyness, you speak loudly to conceal your fears, and put on an overconfident air to mask your insecurities. You are sitting in a mandatory "assembly" to experience a presentation that, as past assemblies have shown, can be a dreadfully boring waste of time. Oh well... At least you're out of class!

Once introduced, usually by the principal, I run out on to the stage, whip off my cowboy hat, and launch right into the truth of the situation. My opening comments are always designed to set an honest tone. "Let's get one thing straight... I did not come here to teach you anything! I came here to learn. What you know about music and life and technology puts to shame the acquired knowledge of my whole lifetime.

Just before we came into this room, I had the opportunity to be in the hallway. I loved watching you and hearing your conversations and whispers as I passed by you. "Who's the old geezer?" you wanted to know. (Much laughter) All the while I was observing you. How you dress, how you look, and how you act. Having done presentations all across the country, I've noticed that young adults and even some teachers had body art. Some of the work was just beautiful. The lines were crisp and the colors were dope. I come from a mostly tattoo-free generation and I wanted to play, too. So, after a story-telling tour across the state of New Jersey, I went home to Las Vegas and found the very finest "INK" artist in Nevada. I had him cover me with age spots. (Showing my arms to much laughter) I ask, "Is he good or what?"

I am a dreamcatcher... That timeless torch that each of us carries. The where I want to go, the what I want to achieve, and the who I want to become. I move on immediately to share with them the process and pathway to my successes and failures, the unvarnished truth about my life and times as it relates to them. I share the highs: the recording artists and stars I have known and promoted, the radio stations I have run, and my exciting work with the Hard Rock organization. I share the lows: that like many of them, I am a molested kid and how, having lost a daughter in a traffic accident, I am aware of their importance to their families, friends, to the world, and now to me.

It simply happens every time... these bright, intuitive young adults realize that we have more in common than they thought when they first saw this old man, and in an instant our forty-five minutes together is gone. Now the six hundred—once rowdy—now and future citizens are on their feet cheering for themselves and their dreams. I have always believed that a speaker is only ever as good as the audience lets us be! What happens after the cheering dies down is my reward for the risk and the effort. High fives and hugs, autographs and stories whispered.

Back at home, mornings always start out with fresh hot coffee and a fresh cold newspaper. The coffee smells dark and rich, with a hint of cinnamon and vanilla. The newspaper always smells of politics. When I created my Executive Training program, "Criteria for Leadership" or C4L as it is known, I mentioned the fact that as we grow, we think we know so many things. My point to executives, both established and emerging, is that knowing is not half as much fun as learning. The Sunday paper is huge, so... although my wife and I read it cover to cover, I set a goal for myself to "find" three things within its pages.

1. Something to help build my business!
2. Something to make me smile!
3. Something to help fill my spirit!

What is amazing and fun is that I usually find all of the above in one spot: the funny papers. Dagwood's wife, Blondie, is building a catering business. Pickles helps me smile about what it will be like when I grow up, and my friend Charles "Sparky" Schulz always reveals the spiritual side of life and loss through his Peanuts characters. Snoopy says, "If you want to be younger... Don't be born so soon!"

Sometimes when our bodies slow down, our minds speed up and allow us to be, as John Denver sang, "All that we can be and not what we are."

Somewhere between the poverty of ignorance and the wealth of imagination...this day is Mine!

PERSONAL JOURNAL

By now, as we think about humor and its heroes, you may have found yourself aghast that I could have forgotten your favorites. Well, that is what this page is for. Look back now and list those performers who brought you the greatest belly laughs. Add your favorite routines to the page. For me, I am thinking Johnathon Winters as "Maude Frickert" and Bob Newhart performing his incredible "King Kong" or "Superman" routines. Continue by adding your favorite funny lines from films and when you run out of those, go out and buy my second book, because I will have already begun a new list, starting with Robin Williams. "Nanu-Nanu!"

"Hey... We don't need no stinking badges!"

CHAPTER TEN
I Will Serve

T oday I will find little ways of giving back. Remembering the times in my life when I was hungry or thirsty for contact or conversation there often appeared, as if by magic, a friend, relative, or neighbor, who found the time or took the time to share an ear or a story with me.

After our daughter was killed in an auto accident many years ago, I would sit on the patio looking out across our lemon orchard and away to the sea. Once, when the emotion was so great that I was simply staring, trying my best to lose track of time and space, I felt a hand touch my arm. When I looked up, the face I saw was not one I knew.

"We are your neighbors," the woman said. "If there is anything we can do, we are here for you." As quickly as she arrived the stranger was gone.

Now fifty years later, that woman and her family are the dearest of friends. Remembering this, it seems that the least I can do is pay the kindness forward. By whatever means, I will make my way to a place where the touch of a hand, the service of a meal, a friendly ear to listen, might just repay the miracles that I have been granted. I will bring my guitar and perhaps my now slightly shaky voice will serve to lighten the darkness of a room or a life. I try hard to remember that folks are always going through something. I don't care how rich or pretty people may appear, they often have challenges that we cannot perceive or imagine. Be kind, thankful, and serve.

He Ain't Heavy, He's My Brother!

My Two Cents...

On the airplane to Canada, my wife broke a nail and wanted it repaired ASAP! It was a cold, snowy day as we crossed the street, heading for the nearest fancy salon. Painfully aware of the decline in great guest/client service throughout the world, I decided to give it another chance. I love to reward excellent service, so I placed a brand new, crisp $100 dollar bill in my shirt pocket. To make it simple, I thought if anyone in this salon was even nice to me, I was going to give them one hundred dollars.

"What do you think?" I asked my wife as we headed for the door. She, being the family bookkeeper, replied, "I think

you're nuts."

Here's the scene. My wife is dressed to the nines and making a Saint John suit look like a million. I am in cowboy boots, hat, rodeo buckle, Wranglers, denim shirt, scarf, and a winter range jacket. I have always wanted to be in a movie and this was my chance.

As we passed through the door, the two reception ladies took one look at us and their jaws dropped. It was obvious that the title to this film was Beauty and the Beast! From that moment on, my wife was treated like diamonds and I was treated like dust.

Throughout the visit during Sharon's nail service, not one person in that salon ever spoke to me. I thought of their dreams, bills, needs, and kids at home, and at holiday time, how important a hundred dollars might be to them. I thought of how close they came to that reward and there but for courtesy, had they missed the opportunity. Even as I pulled out my American Express Platinum card to pay the bill, there was still no "Thank you!"

The chance to serve is a true gift; the more faithful the service, the greater the reward. Whether it is in business or in our personal lives, the caring heart and gentle hand of a family member or friend may be the only kindness that comes to brighten up the day of another. My long-time friend, John Paul DeJoria, the co-founder of John Paul Mitchell systems and the C.E.O. of Patron, is an incredible example of service to humankind and to our planet.

My $100 dollar bill is still folded up in my pocket.

PERSONAL JOURNAL

On this journal page, make a list of at least ten acts of kindness extended to you during your lifetime. You may list as many as you wish but ten must be the minimum. Next, list at least three places that you might contribute to the well being of others in your area.

CHAPTER ELEVEN
I Will Play

T oday I will play once again! We don't quit playing because we get old; we begin to get old the moment we quit playing. Though touch football, marathons, and tennis games may be behind us, the act of playing is the art of empowering our aging. This one day, as Rod Serling's characters did in the Twilight Zone, I will kick the can, play hide and seek, build a fort with my grandkids, pull out the Monopoly and Yahtzee boards, and make plans for sleeping out in my own back yard.

In our times, games were played across a card table from one another and communication was often tin can to tin can across a string. We talked and laughed and from time to time, we cried at the loss of a loved one in the war across the sea. We were the first ones through the gate for the opening of Disneyland and continue to visit every year. Each Easter, we slept out underneath the stars in the Mojave Desert and created our own fireworks magic under the velvet sky.

We need to slow down and take time for these special moments to happen to us now. I realize that for some reason, the ground has become much harder through the years, so I will prepare a proper and comfortable place to rest, out in the open. Each year, in July, I will look up at the fireworks above me, as my nation celebrates its founding across the summer sky. In August, the Perseids meteor shower puts on a show above my home and this year I will sleep out, in comfort, under those stars and become a part of the magic. With the arrival of autumn, I will, for as long as I am able, ride my bike down the street past all those wonderful memories. A bicycle is a time machine that can carry us back through afternoons of falling leaves, freshly cut grass, shortening sunsets, and the flight of the first firefly.

This year, ride out, walk out, and be a part of the harvest moon rise. I will, as my body and spirit allow... play!

S'mores, anyone?

My Two Cents...

"Somewhere out there, beneath the pale moonlight..." *Once again, this summer we will have the opportunity to share in a celestial experience. August is the month of the Perseids Meteor Shower. It is a fresh chance for us to look*

up to the sky and if the night is clear, behold a wondrous sight. NASA suggests that "the Perseids feature fast and bright meteors that frequently leave trails." These magical lights across the sky are the result of tiny dust particles, often no larger than a grain of sand, disintegrating as they enter our atmosphere.

Just before dawn, I plan to face up toward the "Dark Sacred Night," as Louis Armstrong calls it and watch and wait. Be patient and know that I will be out there with you! "It helps to know we might be sleeping 'neath the same dark sky!" Sleeping out in our own backyard is the best and if it rains we can always go inside and build a fort! Can you come out and play?

Do it now. Wouldn't it be tragic to discover at the end of our lives that hot fudge sundaes were really good for us all along?

PERSONAL JOURNAL

On this page make a list of those things that you have done simply for the fun of it. Then add to the list those things you would include on your daily and weekly schedule that would be fun.

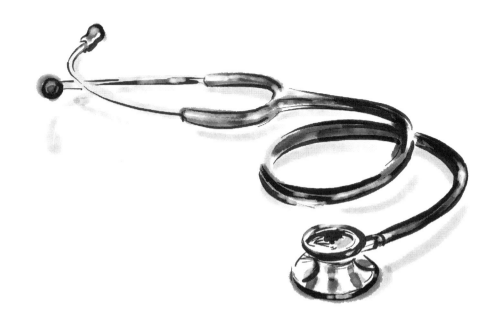

CHAPTER TWELVE
I Will Take My Medicine

Today I will manage my well being! My surfer's face is a skin cancer farm. From basal to squamous cell lesions, I am a poster boy for MOHS surgery! My secret is that I am happy and confident about my future, because I am deeply involved and playing a starring role in managing my health and well being.

I have a phrase that I use to express my feeling of well being: "One Hundred Percent!" Any day that I feel less than "One Hundred Percent," I do something about it! I can change the foods I choose to eat and the beverages I choose to drink. I can increase or decrease the amount of exercise I do and I can be sure each night when I lay my head down that I am truly resting well and healing my body and being. I have some wonderful partners in my health management: my family physician, my dentist, my cardiologist, my dermatologist, and my gastroenterologist! In most cases these friends and physicians don't need to fix anything; they just give me a heads-up on what is going on and what is coming up. They are, for the very most part, preventative partners. So many of the common ailments that claim the lives of our family and friends are easily managed when diagnosed early. I miss "Sheriff Bart" and Jim Henson.

Please don't put it off! Do as I do; set up a complete exam and whatever the results may be, move forward with knowledge, courage, and hope.

You and I need to die young as old as we can!

My Two Cents...

Rx: I am convinced that laughter is truly the best medicine! We all have gonnas, haftas, and wannas! Things that we are going to do, things that we must do, and things that we want to do. They are all important, but today, remember the importance of laughter. For us Sh-Boomers, it's an absolute "Hafta!"

Each day brings challenges. Our family has seen our share of these and we have, more than once, held each other in tears, but we always find our way back to laughter as the medicine that binds us and holds us together. Laughter, deep and hearty, makes us fill our lungs with life-giving oxygen; it quickens our pulse and causes us to communicate at a most rich primal level.

I had a boss recently who suffered an incredible personal loss. Even though we could and did sit and share our grief, we always closed our personal time with a hug and a smile. He and I also shared some great public moments visiting comedy clubs and then, in the days thereafter, recalling and reciting the best material. We took our business and our team members very seriously, but we always found time to laugh ourselves back into good health.

In the nineteen forties, Walt Kelly's Pogo Possum said, "Don't take life so seriously; it ain't no-how permanent." In City Slickers, Billy Crystal's character said, on finding his long lost smile, "It was in Colorado... the last place you always look."

Think of the wonderful funny things that you have seen and heard throughout your lifetime and make them a part of your conscious, current memory. Peter Sellers, Dudley Moore, George Carlin, Kathleen Madigan, and Mitch Hedberg; listen in and laugh yourself to better health.

Remember... age gets better with wine!

PERSONAL JOURNAL

This is a terrific place to make a list of those wellness-related items that may have slipped off your radar. I also like to write about the feeling I get when I step out of my dermatologist or dentist's office, knowing that the treatment/surgery/care that I have received is thorough and complete. For a skin cancer survivor, MOHS is a miracle! I want to know that I am managing my health and that it is not the other way around.

CHAPTER THIRTEEN
Today I Will Walk The Pathway

On my first lecture tour of Australia I had the pleasure of sitting in an airplane seat beside an Aboriginal Tribal Elder. During our conversation, I asked him about the uncanny ability of his people to follow the trail of lost souls in the outback. He smiled and in his beautiful Aussie accent replied, "We don't follow the trail, we send the trail out before us!"

Today I will head out to climb the hill that lies behind our desert home. The City View Trail is a winding gravel path that zig-zags upward toward the crest of the hill. From on high, the view of the Las Vegas valley is astounding. But that is only the cherry on the top of the adventure. The pathway has become my gymnasium, my treadmill, my source of cardiovascular inspiration, my trainer, and more. Because the bed of the path is made of crushed rock and gravel, it is an uneven, slippery slope to manage.

On my first ascent, I found myself sliding, puffing, and pausing frequently, as I struggled to reach the summit. But now, as the months have passed, my breathing and heart rate are smooth and relaxed. (Blood Pressure 112 over 62.) My muscles seem to celebrate the elevation with each step. But wait, there's more! My trail/coach is beginning to strengthen my mind as well. To keep from slipping on the gravel, I find myself looking ahead and focusing carefully on the terrain ahead. My eyes see the obstacles and guide each possible footfall. In doing this, my vision, focus, and mental coordination have improved measurably. My balance is steady and I am confident... mind, body, and spirit... and all for free.

Did I mention that I have lost twenty pounds? What is your pathway to increasing and maintaining health and vigor?

My Two Cents...

Many times in his films, John Wayne refers to the folks who travel through the stories as "pilgrims." Each morning, when I head up my beloved mountain, I feel like a pilgrim. The definition of a pilgrim is a religious devotee, a person who travels to a place of great personal importance, or simply, any wayfarer. Once your "Dreamsheet" is complete and in your pocket, every step you take becomes a pilgrimage.

On my way, I often find revelations of the spirit. The photo at the header of this section was captured early one cold morning on my way to the summit. With the morning sun over my shoulder, I raised my smarter-than-me phone and captured this image.

Afterward I realized that I have never taken a selfie. I've had to look at me for many decades and I know that I would much rather look at you! After all, everything I have ever learned came from listening, watching, and experiencing both the wisdom and foolishness of people just like you. Whether it's John Wayne's Pilgrim, or Fred Roger's Neighbor, I thank you for the journey.

I call this photo a "shelfie..." or a shadow of myself.

Here's looking at you, kid!

PERSONAL JOURNAL

However you travel these days and whatever speed suits you best... use this page to list the spots, places, and adventures that would get you out and about. No excuses here! Remember our friend Jack who had his wheelchair reconfigured so that he could go hunting at his beloved cabin in Wyoming? Whether your pathway leads you to the front porch swing or Mount Kilimanjaro, put it on the list.

CHAPTER FOURTEEN
Coming To Our Senses

Charles Dicken's character Scrooge discovered—with the help of three very persuasive spirits—that he was not, in fact, too old to change. On awakening from his miserable, selfish life, he said, "I haven't lost my senses, I've come to them." He was trying to explain his giddy behavior to his frightened housekeeper. Imagine being such a mean-spirited, bitter soul that those around you live in fear of your presence.

We often speak about our senses. As we age, our perception of the world, through our usual senses, definitely changes. Our once clear vision seems to blur or for some of us, disappear altogether. Our hearing begins to fade at one frequency or another and we find ourselves reaching more frequently for a seasoning that will boost the flavors that once smelled and tasted so aromatic and savory. For those of us with diabetes, we are taught to count on examination, to replace our once acute sense of feeling that told us when a splinter had invaded our feet. These experiences are well known to most of us.

Today, as a Sh-Boomer, there are two other senses that I want to bring to the fore on the common list. Number six is the sense of humor, which we have discussed frequently in the previous pages of this book. Number seven is the sense of wonder. These two are the keys to the gateway of our "Explosion of Joy!" These forgotten favorites, used wisely and patiently, can help fill the void of our other fading senses.

The greatest danger here is our self-talk. Nothing drives out the sense of youthful wonder like the words, "We never do it like that!" "I've always done it this way!" "That never works!" Or perhaps the most debilitating of all, "I've seen everything and I'm just too old for this foolishness!" I want to grow and I need to know. I enjoy watching Nature and NOVA on PBS. The act of expanding my knowledge reduces, logarithmically, the chance of the diminishing of my mind. Roald Dahl's Willy Wonka covered it well when he whispered in Veruca Salt's father's ear, "A little nonsense now and then is relished by the wisest men..."

My Two Cents...

In my life, I have had the great gift of performing onstage in front of large groups of people. One year, at an annual symposium, I was invited to learn, practice, and perform as a part of my inspirational presentation, an illusion for an audience of more than two thousand people. My magic was the creation of fire from within my bare, empty hands. It was not a simple trick and required some days and hours of rehearsal to make it smooth, natural, and convincing. Once onstage, in my red Pendleton mountain man's robe, I told the story of how within each of us dwells a spark that only we ourselves can ignite. I revealed how others may perceive it and wish it for us, but only we can strike the flint and bring the flame to life. I then raised my hands before my face and seemingly out of nowhere produced a flame that rose brightly in the darkness. What a wonderful response from the audience.

At the conclusion of my performance the master magician, who had been my coach and trainer, came to me to share his enthusiasm for my performance. I was flattered to have him ask if I would like to learn some more secrets of the trade. I'm sure that my answer stunned him. I said no thank you for the kind offer, never wanting to lose the sense of wonder as to how an illusion is performed. Our world, through media and technology, has stripped humankind of any remaining sense of mystery. By the time our children, grandchildren, and great grandchildren reach the age of heartbeats and handholding, they have seen every intimate contact, from sexuality to violence and too often in the same graphic piece of video. No thank you.

I am definitely not childish, but I certainly want to preserve forever my "childlike" sense of wonder.

PERSONAL JOURNAL

On this Personal Journal page take the opportunity to use your imagination. Ask yourself, "If I had a Magic Wand, what would I do with my life." Just allow yourself, whatever your personality, to wander and wonder. Begin a list of things that you might do to expand your experience. Perhaps go as far as to think of adventures that you may have avoided in the past for fear of the consequences. Whether you end up doing all of these things is unimportant. It is the act of exploring your absolute sense of wonder that makes this exercise so important and valuable. This is the fountain of youth, Enjoy...

CHAPTER FIFTEEN
Today I Will Be A Friend

Today I am going to promise myself not just to "want a friend," but to "be a friend." Friendship and companionship do not arrive by United Parcel. Friendship, at any age, is born out of an outreach between us. "No matter how far we go or how long it takes for us to get there, once we get there... That's where we are." I think my kid sister was the first one to say that to me.

Well we're here; now what? Loneliness is not a condition of aging. It is often self-imposed. I have both family and friends who, by their own admission, have relatives they would prefer "not" to visit or see. If you find yourself "abandoned," perhaps the problem is not just "them." It may lie within your own stars and approach. It's not too late to grow and change. Whether you are in an assisted living facility or on a jet aircraft headed for some international city of intrigue and entertainment, the truth remains: we all need friends.

It is absolutely true that some of us are more social creatures and some of us are reclusive types, but the older we get, the more often we find ourselves isolated, in both the hope and need of human interaction. In this Sh-Boomer world, distances between family members have grown with the call and need for employment and gainful engagement.

Where to begin? Let's start with forgiveness. Sometimes the most important, powerful tools in a relationship are the hardest to express. I am very aware of those times that my selfishness and ignorance have caused pain to others. I have also learned to take responsibility and then to forgive myself! "I forgive me!" "I forgive you!" "I forgive life!" Just breathe deeply and say it. The act of self-forgiveness begins to open the doorway to new friendships and an end to the curtain of loneliness.

If we are going to be the last generation on the planet to honor the simple virtues of courtesy, kindness, caring, and respect, we need to step up into our leadership roles. After all, we cannot, in good conscience, blame the generations that are so lost in their technology that they cannot look into one another's eyes and speak in whole sentences. I think we need to begin spanking their parents immediately. OMG

To make and keep connections, we need to focus on giving attention, not on getting attention. Perhaps it's time that we stopped expecting love and started giving it!

My Two Cents...

The ball just came rolling down the hill past me, bringing with it memories of baseball with my own kids. I stepped into the street and scooped it up. I could hear the two voices above me yelling, "A little help, please!" Happy to oblige, I wound up and tossed the official major league baseball back to the father and son.

Watching the two throwing the ball back and forth, breaking in the lad's new glove, I was reminded of how important it is to be and stay connected to our loved ones. It isn't always a baseball or football that we toss back and forth. I would add to the list, humor, kindness, gratitude, concern, wisdom, and perhaps most importantly, time! As parents, grandparents, and eventually great-grandparents, all too often we see our roles as talkers, teachers, and preachers. Every bit as important is the role of listener and learner.

When our kids, families, and friends begin to realize that we have truly begun to listen, hear, and learn from them, it opens a whole new doorway to communication!

"We cannot play a good game of catch without keeping our eyes and our focus on each other and the ball!

PERSONAL JOURNAL

You can spark some wonderful memories and ideas on Life Building, by journaling. One of my favorites, is creating and then trying some actions and outcomes, before I light the fuse. Use these pages to list some things that you could do, to simply be a better friend to those you know and those you will come to know. Do not limit your thinking to old friends but include strangers who will come your way in your daily life. Nothing happens by chance.

CHAPTER SIXTEEN
The Secret Power Of Kindness

It seems that we love our super heroes. We are fascinated by beings who look a bit like us but seem to have powers beyond our own. Each of my now grown offspring have their own chosen super heroes, ranging from Super Woman and The Hulk to Mighty Mouse. The box office receipts in these two centuries seem to prove my point: that we are truly enthralled with these imaginary characters.

I have some wonderful news for you: We are blessed with just such a power, the gift of kindness. Immediately, those of us with our macho motor running insert the word weakness where kindness was printed, and those of us blessed with a touch of the feminine side smile broadly and recognize the immense power of the word and the acts performed under its banner. Often times, more than doing something, kindness is a way of holding someone in your thoughts or in your heart. Every "please" and "thank you" is an act of kindness. Every moment spent listening with respect to the elders and youngest of our tribe is a kindness. Every outreach to lift up and help another is an act of kindness. I don't hold doors open because the woman or man behind me is weak or incapable; I do it because courtesy and kindness were a part of my upbringing, and more importantly, it feels good to me. More than once I have found myself on top of a contentious boardroom situation by simply showing a little genuine kindness.

I have always tried to be the father worthy of my children's honor.

My Two Cents...

I write a weekly newsletter titled, "The Desert Wind." Some time ago, I wrote about the Loggerhead Shrike parents who came to live in one of the cacti just up the hill from our home. These beautiful, confident birds got used to my visits and eventually allowed me to meet and photograph their offspring in their well-built nest. From eggs to flight, I shared their emerging life. I was touched that those baby birds had imprinted on my presence to the point that once in flight, they came to spend time near our patio whenever they heard my voice.

It gets better. It turns out that these two young birds were coming to build their own nest in our bush and to raise their own brood under our watchful eyes and protection.

We were sharing three generations of wildlife.

On my morning visit today, the fledgling, shown above, posed for me on the edge of the nest as if to say, "I am getting ready to fly, Cowboy!"

For both human and wild creatures it can sometimes be a tough and harsh world. May we all touch those we bring into the world and those creatures with whom we share this wonderful planet with kindness. It costs us nothing to interact with kindness and wisdom. Often, that is all it takes to give wings to their dreams.

PERSONAL JOURNAL

Use this page to collect your thoughts and recollections of people who have shared their kindness and caring with you. I like to use the journalists investigative style and think: Where, when, what, who and how you were blessed. One of the great acts of kindness is a simple, sincere "Thank you!" This is your opportunity to make the list, the commitment and the connection with these friends both past and present and reach out to them with remembrance and gratitude.

CHAPTER SEVENTEEN
Beautiful Beginnings

It has taken me a long time to realize it, but I just love beautiful beginnings. I find that I no longer have room in my life for sad or bitter endings! How we begin it often gives clues as to how we will end it. That doesn't mean that everything always works out the way I want it or that I am never touched by disappointment and sadness; it just means that today I handle things in a much different and better way. Somewhere along the way I must have shifted my mind, because nothing much has changed around me. The Seven Dwarves still exist—Happy, Grumpy, Sneezy, Doc, Sleepy, Bashful, and Dopey—and they all still shop at Wal-Mart. I am just a bit more careful in choosing which characters are worthy of my time.

I have also discovered that I can do the very same thing with my thoughts! I have simply put my hands firmly back on the wheel of the one thing of which I have command and that is me, my life, and I. Each evening when I go to my repose, I remove my "imaginary" special glasses, gently close my eyes, and begin the practice of remembering. Call it meditation or contemplation, it is just my way of connecting my wonderful, curious little world with the infinite universe. Instant replay worked in our minds before television used it to divert our attention from the fact that a real live game had broken out, right in front of us. I love this real life that has broken out right in front of me. I fall asleep with my favorite moments in my mind's eye, and hold them gently in my mysterious subconscious. Each morning as I awaken, I slip on my special pair of glasses. That is all it takes to change the way I view the world.

My Two Cents...

For me, each day seems to bring a time for beautiful beginnings and promises. My favorite line from Charles Dickens, A Christmas Carol, is recited during Scrooge's awakening to the power of his attitude and actions and how they had affected his days and would surely influence his future. Scrooge, having been both terrified and enlightened by the three spirits, awakens on Christmas day back in his room to declare, "It's not too late. I haven't missed it!"

My beautiful beginning or resolution is more of a revolution, a willingness to change not only the direction of my life, but the quality of my living as well. Remember that Ebenezer Scrooge proclaimed he would change if he could, but he could not. "I'm too old to change!" he wailed. Not so for him and not so for us.

Before I promise others, I realize that I must promise myself: I promise myself physically, financially, emotionally, and spiritually, to be just a bit better with each day of my life. I open my heart to the people and the possibilities that come my way.

I work without fear, by seeing the good that others don't see, doing those things that others won't do, and believing when others cannot.

I enjoy the journey, by recognizing my life to be a process, not a problem... I am living an adventure.

I reach out with my spirit, by contributing to the world around me in both intention and action. And I do this when no one is watching.

When I created my little book, This Day is Mine, in which these thoughts were born, I was awakening from my past to joyfully discover that, "It was, in fact, not too late, I hadn't missed it!"

If sunrise is the beginning, then sunset must be the beginning of the beginning!

PERSONAL JOURNAL

On this page make a list of those things that have proven to be precursors to the best and worst adventures of your life. Think, "Been there-Done that!" We are not building a wall to prevent exploration, but simply reviewing flags of experience that will help guide us into beautiful beginnings!

CHAPTER EIGHTEEN
I Will Create

Every one of us has a talent, often hidden, rarely recognized, and sometimes lying inside like a sleeping giant. I make found object art. "Found object art" is a marketing term for putting sticks together into statues. Truly, I look for and collect beach driftwood and windblown desert treasures that, over time, begin to take shape in my imagination and then I fashion them into pieces of art. The photograph that accompanies this chapter, is titled, "His Morning Song." It sits on our patio, facing the rising sun. I do this because I am limited to drawing stick people. At least I can make stick artwork.

When we were younger, we all tried so many different

creative things. We gave a shot at drawing, painting, writing, playing an instrument, or singing. For many of us, our foray into the arts was met with negative commentary from both friends and family. These painful observations often turned us away from those things we once thought to try. "You will never make it as a sax player!" "Is that the best horse you can draw?" "You must be tone deaf. You better not try to sing!" Negative comments like these can add up to a heavy dose of discouragement and put us off of a lifetime of creating.

Having met a lot of people around the world, I have never met a person who honestly had no talent. I'm not sure whether it was talent or sheer determination, but in my time I have written a hit song and sung the theme song in a movie.

Often the best place to begin is with writing. Throughout this book, if you have been getting your money's worth, you have been creating a journal, both historical and prophetic. You have been corresponding with yourself in very important terms. You have said, "I like this, I don't like that, I want this, I don't want that, I will do this and I will no longer do that." You have examined your past and present and have begun the process of authoring the guidelines for your future. The document is called a "Dreamsheet..." and it will be your sky-chart for a Sh-Boom journey going forward.

We can always say, "I can't do that, I don't know how or I've never been able to do that." Try again: Sing, draw, write, paint, take photos, make something, but for heaven's sake, as Momma Cass sang so beautifully, "make your own kind of music." Who knows? You might even turn a simple stick into a piece of history.

My Two Cents...

Stick: A surf board, a hard tackle, an obstructionist or maybe...just a simple piece of cedar wood! Some years ago, I was invited to do a mainstage presentation for one of my fine client companies. I knew that the audience would be composed of about two thousand true professionals from all around the world and I wanted to share something for them to carry home as a reminder of our time together. From a large piece of cedar on our ranch, I split the sweet smelling wood into small pieces. It took a while to whittle out one of these little rascals for each guest, but by the end of the day I was ready for the Symposium. When our guests arrived for my presentation, there was a small piece of cedar, just big enough to hold in your hand, placed on every seat in the showroom. Those fragrant pieces were a reminder that wherever we may go, "We Ride Together!" One of these cedar treasures was picked up at the symposium by the great chemist and executive Paul Premo and was re-gifted to me twenty years later. At a recent dinner, Arthur Long, a true international master/ executive, brought forth his "stick" and shared our story with the dignitaries in attendance.

We get out of life exactly what we put into it. Whatever you choose to create becomes an extension of yourself. Whether your intention is to create for your own enjoyment or to share your gift with the world is your call. Just do it! I still carry my fragrant cedar reminder of those moments shared...

As promised...

DREAMSHEET GUIDELINES and PERSONAL JOURNAL

The Dreamsheet discipline is a formalizing of your heart's deepest desires. It is a simple, thought provoking, joyful experience. What you are about to do will profoundly change your life, your actions, and your ability to achieve what may have once seemed nearly impossible.

To begin, sit quietly and think about your life as it is, as it has been, and how you would like it to become. Then, write down in very simple language those things that you most want to accomplish with your life. At first, don't be concerned about how many, how much, or what parts of your life the dreams include; just write! To begin the first entry on the top of the page, use the words, "My Dream Is." Always use the same phrase, "My Dream is," when you begin to describe or discuss your desires, either internally or with trusted others.

When you are ready to refine and define your dreams, break them down into four categories as follows:

Physical: The thing or things that you want to attain. During your reflective times, visualize the following: Wellness, living quarters, surroundings, responsibilities, and things that you need or want to acquire. What do these things look like to you?

Financial: What amount of income do you need-want going into the future? If you are on a fixed income, ask yourself how you could more wisely use the money that you currently receive and what ideas you have for creating additional income to strengthen your position and build on your future. If you are still employed save, save, save!

Emotional: How do you want to feel about life, as opposed to how you feel about life right now? What thoughts and actions would help to replace your negative feelings, like sadness and anger, with a bit more happiness and joy?

Spiritual: My youngest son, Chris, once said to me, "Dad, I get the physical, financial, and emotional, but when you say spiritual, my TV screen gets a little fuzzy." My response was and is that anything in your life of which you cannot take a picture is in the realm of spiritual. Love for another, love for your family, respect for the earth, a reverence for your chosen faith, the feeling that you get when the first breath of spring blows across your face... all of these can be felt in the heart and perceived in the spirit, but they cannot be photographed. There is an eternal place in each of us that knows instinctively when something is right. It matters not that you have never embraced these ideas before. Begin now!

Every dream or goal is, or should be, a bit of all four. I choose the name "Dreams" as opposed to "Goals," because goals will become the footsteps that we follow on our journey, but it is always the power of the Dream that re-awakens the energy needed to achieve our dreams! Throughout the days and years, your dreams will grow and change. Each time the process will be the same.

Once the process is completed, fold your "Dreamsheet" carefully and keep it with you at all times. It is a scientific fact that close proximity to powerful information alters our being, sharpens our focus, and empowers our will to achieve. Never "board the day" without your flight plan! Hold it close in a purse, pocket, or wallet and you will always be the "keeper of your dreams."

May this be the beginning of many Dreams Come True. You can do it. In fact, only you can do it!

Those who see the invisible can achieve the impossible!

Peace, Blessings, and Dreams Come True...

SH-BOOM!

I try hard to remember that what we are doing in the art of "dream-sheeting," is not just planning out positive endings but also truly enjoying the process of stepping into beautiful beginnings. So let this not be the ending of your Sh-Boom days but the start of re-reading both your entries and the words that I have crafted as an author. Make it your habit to master the art of journaling. Keep dreaming and keep adding to the pages ahead. Remember: the words and pictures contained in this book, will become your positive, powerful legacy to those who follow in your footsteps.

CONTACT DOUG
Email: Doug@DougCoxOnline.com

To find more books and audiobooks by Douglas A. Cox, including his best seller, "This Day Is Mine," please visit **www.DougCoxOnline.com** and follow him on Facebook: **www.facebook.com/dougcoxonline**

ABOUT THE AUTHOR

Douglas A. Cox is a twenty-first century dreamcatcher! As an internationally known inspirational speaker, his presentations have touched and enlightened audiences throughout the world. Songwriter, singer, performer, and storyteller par excellence, Doug is passionate, funny, and entertaining. His home is on the edge of the southwestern desert of Nevada, where he lives with his wife and their world famous author and cat, "Three O'clock On The Nose." Doug's love for nature is expressed through his world renowned photography, in which he captures the secrets of both the beauty of flowers and the creatures hiding in them. As Doug says, "I'm a Cowboy who surfs!" He then adds, "Do you have any idea how hard it is to keep your horse on the board?"

"Doug, Your kind words came on a dark day and lifted me as nothing else could. A friend at first sight..."
Dr. Gerald Mann, friend and Sh-Boomer

"I came to this seminar not knowing what to expect. From the first moment Doug began to speak, it was as if a light came on for me... for all of us! We came together and the fun, the happiness, the rich feelings, and the common bond of understanding of our time in life poured out onto us and into us. It was no less than an Explosion of Joy!"
Jim Ahlquist, friend and Sh-Boomer

"Doug's understanding of the human spirit is unrivaled; his ability to unleash its awesome power is legendary!"
Neil Ducoff, publisher, friend, and Sh-Boomer

Made in the USA
Lexington, KY
27 February 2017